Learn Corporate Culture And Boost Your Career

By

Clive Verrall

Preface

This book is for people with ambition that want to succeed in the corporate workplace.

Are you making the most of the opportunities available to you? You can see that working for a corporation can be more rewarding financially and professionally for some people than for others. Do they know something that the rest of the employees don't?

You may have excellent colleagues that can't understand why they haven't had the breaks, while watching other people overtake them. Some people will have plateaued in their career or seem to be out of favor, do you know what happened to them?

In this book are key lessons about corporate life that you can learn now. Aimed at both those people already in the corporate world and those looking to join from smaller organizations. There are detailed explanations of what to expect, which types of people you are likely to meet, navigating company politics, how promotions work and how to survive major changes. Finally, the book explains how you might move on to your next corporate position.

All the explanations in this book come from the practical experiences of real people working in this environment for the last 30 years. I will share years of knowledge, facts, and inside advice with you from daily life to corporate mergers so that you may succeed in your chosen corporate career.

Find out more in this book about the often unmentionable subject of office politics. However hard-working and intelligent you are, the office politics around you can derail your career. Learning how this is possible could help you from falling into a trap later on. Do not underestimate how dangerous office politics can be.

Help yourself by learning more about how corporations work. This book will help you gain the inside track and boost your career.

Acknowledgments

The author would like to express his gratitude to the following people for spending their time reviewing the book and providing comprehensive feedback. Without their good-will, patience and hard work this book would not be as it is today.

Name	Location
Durga Shanker Pandey	India
Fancois Brault	France
Isaure Venite-Rossi	Canada
James Barker	Thailand
Jatinder Seehra	United Kingdom
Krishna Reddy Vennavaram	India
Paul Simion	Singapore
Renaud de Villemeur	Canada
Shashikant Bhushan	Singapore
Simon Ward	United Kingdom
Sujata Dabhole	United Kingdom

Table of Contents

Prepare yourself for the long term 7

Advancement 8

People 8

Aim for promotion 10

Essential facts about career appraisals....................18

Setting goals.. 21

Setting goals retroactively 22

Motivation - carrot and stick 24

How to start networking 26

When to say "no" to extra work............................. 30

Can I be absent from work?.....................................32

What training is available to me? 36

Knowing more about compensation 40

Regular reorganizations 41

Surviving mergers and acquisitions 42

Raising concerns with your manager........................ 46

Hard truth about raising grievances 48

Whistle blowing... 50

How being mentored can help you............................ 51

Increasing your value to the organization.................52

How office politics can affect you..............................57

When office politics become toxic........................ 58

Toxic office politics checklist 63

Crossing the Rubicon to management 65

Get recognized as a manager 65

Learn new skills 67

Managing within your sphere of knowledge 68

Managing in a new area 68

Moving on 70

Always be prepared for change 70

Reasons for leaving 73

What is a better opportunity? 75

How to survive the redundancy process 77

Conclusion 81

About the Author 83

Prepare yourself for the long term

Whether you joined the corporation as a fresh graduate or as a professional hire, after a few years you will find your early advantage behind you. To make that next step forward you need to understand more about how corporations work and then use that information to improve your position. This chapter will help you.

A career is usually measured in decades not in weeks or months. Whatever stage you are at in your career it is essential to be prepared for the long term. Actions you take today may not deliver fruit immediately, it may take months or years. Preparing for the long term will increase the chances of career advancement when the opportunities arise.

Advancement

Corporates are competitive places. At any point in time, your colleagues could be chasing all the opportunities while you are left behind doing the work. Try to identify the difference between there being no relevant opportunities for you at the moment and reaching a career plateau where new opportunities will rarely arise.

At any point in your career, you may feel that nothing new or exciting has happened for a while and you have reached a plateau. This often happens with people who want to become specialists because they reach a point where there is no clear next move upwards while remaining a specialist. If you prefer to specialize then that may be okay for you.

Otherwise, if you see yourself on the management career path then you don't want to plateau. Always be ready for opportunities and aim for promotion.

People

Get to know your manager better. Try to understand his motivation, what is he looking for, what seems to please him. You don't need to become best of friends with him but it can help you a lot to understand his point of view. One aspect of this is to get to know more about his boss and what he expects of him.

Find allies within the organization. Your allies could be your friends who work in other parts of the organization or they could just be people that you have helped and they want to return the favor. With allies, you are looking for people that can help you when needed. Otherwise, your scope of influence will be no bigger than the team you are in and if you wish to leave that team then you may be completely unsupported outside.

Ideally, your allies will act as unofficial character witnesses when anyone mentions you or asks what you are like.

It is always a good strategy to also have good relationships with some people outside your management hierarchy. A particularly important group of people to pay attention to are the personal assistants of the senior managers. These people control access to the manager and if they like you then they are more likely to tell you where he is or to squeeze you into his schedule for a 5-minute chat when you need it. Furthermore, many managers ask the opinion of their assistants when they want to know more about a person. So having a good relationship helps.

Learn to tolerate and be patient with people that you don't like. One way or another you all have to work together. Don't hold a grudge. The person you dislike may become your boss, or you become his boss. Keep it cordial and professional.

Be aware that even within the same team as you, the efficiency and productivity of each person will differ wildly. Getting a large team of people to work together is very inefficient compared to one expert working on their own. Even the productivity of one plus one rarely equals two. However, this is the model chosen by large corporates. The best you can do is to notice who does what within the team and who can help you.

Similarly, the profile of the managers you will meet in a corporate will vary a great deal too. organizations will always have a few very good managers, lots of average managers and some poor managers. Often the poor managers are people who lack the skills to manage or have been passed over for promotion so many times that they are now demotivated beyond repair. Then there are managers you will meet who will leave you wondering if they are really managers or if they are politicians. They may lack team and task management skills but their ability to manage upward to senior management ensures they are always seen in a good light.

A good manager will do his best to create an environment in which his team can thrive. This may mean protecting them from company politics, putting pressure on other teams to deliver what you need or fighting for the resources your team needs.

Your research into the people and culture of the organization should never stop. People are a very important part of working in a big corporation.

Aim for promotion

All of us who join a major corporation are looking for career growth or career progression. In my many years of employment, I could count on one hand the number of people I have met who had no ambition at all for their role to evolve. One of the reasons for this is that there are many ways to consider career progress and growth. This may include the following.

- Improved job title
- Increase in compensation
- Going up in the organization chart
- Higher company ranking/classification
- Having a bigger budget
- Increased autonomy
- Managing more people
- Moving to a prosperous area
- Changing country or city

People often talk about "climbing the corporate ladder". This refers to one type of career progression where there is an imaginary path from your entry point in the organization up to being the head of the corporation. In practical terms, if someone works for a support function then instead of climbing the ladder to become the head of the corporation it is more likely to be interpreted as becoming the head of their particular support function, e.g. starting as an accounting clerk and aiming to become the Chief Financial Officer.

In some corporations, this path has defined steps. They will have a corporate grading scheme where each employee is assigned to a particular level in the organization which corresponds to a particular rung on the ladder for that corporation. In many other corporations, the job title illustrates where a person is in the corporation and where they could move to next; e.g. if someone is junior vice president then they know that the next promotion will take them to vice president, director and then managing director. In some other organizations, the job titles give little indication of where they are in the hierarchy. In which case to see the ladder it is necessary to look at the current organization chart to see which roles there are between the person's current position and the top of the organization chart.

Alternatively, there are other employees who also want career growth but they don't see themselves as ever running the corporation or being the head of their service function. For example, in the Information Technology department, there may be people who want to become experts in their own technical field and they want to be recognized for it but they don't want to become the head of the department. They don't see themselves on the traditional corporate ladder but they are still looking for opportunities and promotions.

How far you can go on the specialist or alternative path often depends whether your role is part of the core business of your employer. For example, in a pharmaceuticals company there will be very high profile roles for the top research scientists. However, an open source technology expert will not have many alternative career path options in a retail bank.

In conclusion, we have identified two different career paths: the traditional path of climbing the corporate ladder and the alternative path of receiving recognition for specialist skills that are not on the traditional corporate ladder.

The people on both the traditional and the alternative career paths would be pleased to receive an improved job title. In the traditional case, the improved job title would reflect climbing further up the corporate ladder and in the alternative case, the job title would increase their recognition as a specialist.

Compensation increases may or may not be synchronized with an improved job title or advancement up the career ladder. Sometimes compensation increases occur unexpectedly because the corporation has realized that the compensation being paid within their organization for specific roles is so much less than that being paid on the market that they feel that a group of their employees are at risk of defecting to their competitors. There are other organizations with a strict grading system where it would not be possible to increase someone's grade without increasing their compensation; which may require a budget increase approval. They may also have strict rules stating what the maximum and minimum increase must be.

Being seen to go up in the organization chart is directly analogous to the traditional notion of climbing the corporate ladder. Those seeking alternative career paths would be less interested in this type of progression unless the improvement is within a specialist part of the organization chart.

Managing more people does not infer an immediate increase in corporate grade or even going up in the organization chart. Many experts say that the number of people you manage is not related to your importance within the corporation or directly related to your compensation and that these are outdated notions. In my experience, being given the chance to manage more people is a long term lever towards climbing the corporate ladder. That is to say that even though your title or your compensation is unlikely to change immediately, in the long term it will be recognized that you are performing a more important role for the organization than you were before and therefore your title, compensation, and grade will increase over time.

Moving to a dynamic new business area could become a catalyst for career growth. If you are a salesperson and you move to an area of the business that is positioned to hugely increase in revenue then your compensation could dramatically increase by joining that area and being successful. This could be described as a sideways move because it does not involve immediately climbing the corporate ladder but it could well lead to faster growth later on. If your long term interest is more about climbing the ladder than immediately increasing your compensation then this type of move has its risks.

For example, if people think you have become successful not through your own endeavors but just because you were carried along by the area that you are in then you might not be recognized for promotion that quickly. Alternatively, if you learn a lot from the experience then senior management may recognize that you could bring similar success to other areas if you were given the opportunity.

Sometimes, changing managers can create the boost that your career needs. Learn about other managers within the organization. You may have contact with a particularly encouraging and knowledgeable manager; when you talk more you may find that he has a position open. Managers are only human and many of them can get the best out of certain people and not others. Can you see a better match for you than with your current manager?

Changing the country or the city in which you work for the corporation could become a leap up the corporate ladder, a good long term sideways move or a very interesting experience that doesn't immediately help your prospects. It very much depends on the circumstances of the assignment. Global corporations employ local staff in their operations around the world but they often want to have a number of people who bring the headquarters corporate culture to the local operation too. This means that there are often opportunities for middle managers to move to another location where they will become the head of their department, this is an excellent career opportunity as it allows the person to demonstrate that they can run a department and they should expect to be promoted when they return.

In my experience, the factors most affecting getting a promotion (of the traditional or alternative kind) are:

- Completing all your tasks well
- Getting noticed
- Showing capacity to do more

There would never be any discussion about

promotion if you couldn't complete all the tasks that were assigned to you. This is the minimum that anyone could ask. If your list of tasks is quite diverse then I might rewrite this first factor as needing to complete all your high profile tasks well. That is to say, if people widely know that you are responsible for certain things then these are the activities that must be completed well and on time to keep and grow your good name.

Consider any personal regulatory compliance tasks to be very high profile. You may be asked to do something mind-numbing that is a distraction from your main tasks, but failing to complete these tasks will be career limiting.

Unfortunately, it is possible to work hard and deliver all your tasks year after year without getting promoted. To escape this situation you need to get noticed. This may seem selfish but your manager and any internal clients need to know that it was you and your teams that achieved these successes. This is where you also need a healthy relationship with your manager, he needs to feel that he can congratulate you in public for your achievements and that by doing that it will reflect well on him too. If he sees you as a threat then he may not want people to know what you have achieved.

If your manager does feel threatened by you, and perhaps you feel that you are better than him, then you need to think very carefully what your next steps will be to get that promotion that you are after. There is an old saying that you should always look after your manager and he will look after you. Approaching people above your manager can be very dangerous for your career, your manager will have many more opportunities than you to explain himself to his manager and in contrast, you may only get one chance. Console yourself with the thought that most people leapfrog their managers on the career ladder through some clever sideways moves, not by taking their role or by becoming their boss.

If you are completing all your tasks and everyone who matters knows about it, but you are still not getting promoted; then question whether people believe you have the capacity to do more than you are. If you get everything done well and yet you regularly make a drama about how hard it has been, how you don't really have the necessary resources or how many extra hours you have had to put in each day then it is unlikely that people will think you have extra capacity. I am not suggesting that you hide the extra hours you have worked or that you keep quiet about the resourcing problems, but you may need to re-frame how you communicate these points.

When you are offered a promotion, by definition, it will be to do something different from what you are already doing. For example, you might be asked to manage the team you are already in or take over an area that everyone knows is in trouble. Regardless of the situation, you will have no real choice but to accept the promotion and then make the most of it. If you say no, then you may not be asked again.

Essential facts about career appraisals

The HR department in every major corporation will run a career appraisal program every year (or perhaps even more often). Depending on the organization this process may be called:

- Career appraisal
- Performance review
- Career assessment
- Personal review
- Appraisal

Despite the use of different names, the purpose of the career appraisal process will be similar at each organization. Your performance since the last appraisal will be evaluated against the company's goals, the personal goals your manager set, and the criteria considered important for your current job role. The outcome of the appraisal should feed directly into the HR driven compensation review.

As part of this process, you will be invited to an appraisal meeting with your manager. During this meeting, you will get to see his evaluation of your performance and goals. Normally there is also a narrative section in the form where your manager can write how he feels you have performed throughout the year. This will allow him to include subjects outside of the goals that were set. This is important because if your responsibilities have shifted during the year then the evaluation of the goals may not be enough to fully represent your activities.

Depending on the organization there may also be other sections on the form which could include an evaluation of how your performance matched with the company's core values, or an evaluation of your skills compared with a standard set of skills expected for your role.

At the end of the appraisal meeting, your manager will explain the goals that he has set you for the next appraisal period. If you think his goals are not relevant or don't fully represent what you believe you are going to do then this is the moment to raise your concerns and discuss the alternatives. A good manager will welcome your input on setting your goals even if he politely rejects your suggestions.

Not all managers, or all appraisal processes, are the same. You may get the opportunity to comment on how you feel the year was for you at any point during the appraisal meeting or you may only get one specific opportunity to speak. If the appraisal meeting is not an open discussion then I suggest you jot down any of the points that you disagree with so that you can be sure to speak about them at the end of the appraisal or to include them in a written summary that you send to your manager if there is no opportunity during the meeting.

If you disagree with your manager's evaluation of your performance then you need to speak up. Many managers are very busy and they grade people based on their gut instincts. If you have been given a particularly bad grade for something, then ask your manager how he reached his conclusion. Review the objective given to you using the SMART model (explained further in the "setting goals" section) and use it to drive your questioning. For example, does this grade reflect a particular measurement that has been taken? The intention is not to start an argument or to show how confident you are but to get to the real thinking behind the grades and to get past any lazy management grading.

Once the appraisal meeting is over you will get the opportunity to prepare your response to the appraisal. This response will be kept as part of the appraisal record. You will need to accept or reject the appraisal for the process to be complete. If you are very unhappy then you can ask your manager for another appraisal meeting to discuss specific points or if you don't feel quite so strongly then you can use your official response to add the context that you believe is missing.

If you find that you cannot resolve your differences with your manager after a second appraisal meeting and you are not prepared to sign the appraisal as it is, then the next stage is to escalate your issues to your HR representative. This is a serious action to take and therefore should only be done if you feel very strongly. If you know that you are not going to win the argument then it may be better to use your official response to explain your situation and to leave it at that.

The appraisal process is complete when every staff member has had at least one appraisal meeting and both the staff member and the manager have signed the appraisal form.

I have seen many managers treat the appraisal process as a waste of their time that they are obliged to do every year. Unfortunately, this can rub-off onto their staff and it is possible to take the attitude that the appraisal doesn't really matter because my manager doesn't think it really matters. At the beginning of my career, I was lucky to be warned about the importance of the appraisal process by colleagues who had had problems with their managers at previous organizations. Their advice to me was that the appraisal is one of the few recorded and signed documents between you and your manager that states categorically what you did that year and how well you did it. When problems arise then the HR department, an internal auditor, a tribunal or a court of law will take these documents very seriously. I suggest you take the same advice.

To protect yourself, it is a good idea to keep your own copy of the appraisal form and any goals that were set that were not entered on the form (this is often the case for new joiners or people changing roles). Do not rely on the HR team to keep records and certainly don't rely on any electronic appraisal system. I have heard many times of online appraisal systems being upgraded and access to all previous appraisals being lost.

Setting goals

Your manager should set you specific goals to achieve during your appraisal that need to be achieved before the next career appraisal. These goals should be a direct reflection of what you understand your main work should be for the following year. Each goal should be specific, measurable, SMART. Of course, that is the theory, your manager may not be that good at setting SMART goals in which case you can offer an alternative phrasing for these goals if it is going to help you.

- SMART goals are:
- Specific
- Measurable
- Assignable
- Realistic
- Time related

During the appraisal process, the goals that were previously set by your manager will be evaluated. Your performance at each of the goals will be graded and comments will be recorded to explain the grades.

Setting goals retroactively

The previous sections assume an ideal world where everyone has the correct goals and that the appraisal meeting follows the correct process. Unfortunately, this doesn't always happen. Let us consider some common issues.

You don't have any goals set from a previous appraisal

Your goals don't match what you have been asked to do that year

The best solution to both of these problems is to actively check your goals each quarter to see if they are aligned with the work you have been doing. If they don't match then speak with your manager and ask to change them.

If you were transferred from another team part way through the year then your new manager should have set your goals when you joined. Follow up with him if this doesn't happen in the first few days.

Assuming that this wasn't possible and only the day before your appraisal meeting you find that the official goals that were set for your are no longer relevant then the most likely outcome is that your manager will attempt to define your goals retroactively during the appraisal meeting. This can be unfair because he both sets the goals and gives you your scores in the same meeting without giving you the chance to deliver against the new goals. Also, you don't get the opportunity to research your own answers.

When you know that you don't have goals set then the best tactic is to write your own goals before the meeting. If you have time then send these goals to your manager by email in advance. Otherwise you can present them during the meeting.

During the times that your manager has not set goals before your meeting it is more likely to be because he is disorganized than that he has a hidden agenda to give you a bad appraisal. Give him the benefit of the doubt. The goals you wrote are likely to be accepted by your manager or at least they will influence the goals that he writes.

After the meeting, if you feel that your appraisal was unnecessarily negative due to the goals that he set retroactively then ask for a new meeting to discuss your issues. Remember that the appraisal is not complete until you have both given your approval to what was written.

Motivation - carrot and stick

In simple terms, your employment by a corporate is a mutual agreement between you and your employer. You get compensated for your time and the corporate gets things done that allow it to continue to make money. In practice, the corporate has a large number of employees from which it needs solutions and deliveries over a long period of time. These same employees have good days and bad days, they have career aspirations and most have financial pressures outside the office (home loans, school fees, etc).

The long term ultimate motivator of the corporate is that next year will be better for you than this year as long as you trust in the system and smash the goals given to you. When you know that there are thousands of people in the organization with job roles that you would like (both in terms of job function and compensation) then you will believe that what you are being offered is achievable. This is the carrot the corporate is dangling in front of you. For example, if you take up extra responsibility immediately after a compensation review then don't expect your compensation to suddenly increase. The corporate expects you to trust your employer enough to wait for the proper time for your compensation increase.

A metaphorical "carrot" is always paired with a metaphorical "stick". The corporate punishment "stick" is that you will lose your job. At the beginning of your career with the corporate, you might not mind too much if you lose your job, after all, you just landed this job and so why couldn't you find another job that is just as good? So at this stage, the fear of the "stick" may not be that much.

The fear of losing your job slowly creeps up on you as time goes by.

The longer you work for this corporate the more effective the "stick" becomes. When you have been working there for some years then you will have become personally invested in that company. If you move on then the goodwill investment that you have made (e.g. the network you have built and knowledge about their business) will be lost. Worse still, you have made a big financial commitment (like buying a house) and you need the monthly employment income to continue to pay the bills. You may have some part of your compensation (perhaps a bonus) paid one year in arrears that you will lose if you leave. Also, you will have been out of the job market for a long time by then, so your interview skills could be rusty and you may have no idea how easily you can find another job.

You can now see how fear of losing your job can become a major influencing factor for many people at a corporate. Many people will still be coming to work to do their job even if they see no improvement on the horizon for their own situation. At this point, the carrot no longer works but the stick is very effective.

Prepare yourself by not falling into this trap.

How to start networking

It will help you to get to know as many people as possible within the corporation. Depending on your role you may or may not get the chance to meet with different people during the working day. The first people to network with are the same people that you work with every day. Building relationships with them will make it easier to do your day to day job.

Your role may require working with people outside of your immediate team from time to time. These may be people that you need to "cross-sell" with (work together to sell their products) or they may be people that you will need services or professional advice from. The best advice is to network with these people before you need their help urgently. When you need them to do something for you then it will be a lot smoother if you already have a good relationship with them.

The third good reason for networking is that you will be new to the organization and your career path may not be in a straight line. By getting to know other people outside of your immediate scope of work you will dramatically increase the number of possible sideways moves in the corporation. If you are young and ambitious then it will be easier for another team to accept you as a new senior member or as their team leader if they already know you and respect you. Managing people that you have never met before can be challenging for an inexperienced manager.

There are many ways to network while working in a corporation. Here are some possibilities.

- Joining people for coffee
- Sitting with people at lunch
- Town hall meetings
- Sports and cultural events
- Company barbecues
- Internal training

Coffee breaks and lunch breaks are a good opportunity to invite someone to join you and then to get to know them a little bit better. To entice them you may find yourself paying for their coffees but it will be a small investment to make in order to build good relationships and to increase your network.

A Town Hall meeting is typically a large meeting with hundreds of people in an auditorium. It is often thought of as a very one-sided communication as the speaker talks and everyone else listens. Despite this, a town hall meeting can also be used to increase your network. First of all, the people speaking at the Town Hall are often important people that you rarely get to meet. Listen to what they say, and then pose questions in public during the meeting (if time is allotted for this), or ask them questions in the coffee break or even approach them days later with your questions. This will get you noticed by them and help you to build relationships. Alternatively, lots of other people attend the Town Hall meeting in the audience with you. Ask them what they thought about what was said, get to know them this way.

The corporation may organize sports and cultural events. This could include a painting competition, holding a badminton tournament, a charity run or having a soccer team. If you are already fairly good at these activities then you can join the corporate event. This is an opportunity to meet people from other departments that otherwise you would have no reason to meet with. Knowing these people could be useful at any point in your career, you just don't know who you are going to meet and how you might help each other.

A sports and cultural event can also be a social leveling experience. For example, a friend of mine was part of the company's soccer club and he regularly remarked that even senior managers came to the soccer training sessions. While they were there they no longer behaved as the boss, but as equal members of the wider soccer team. This made it easier to approach them and to build relationships with them.

Don't get me wrong. I am not advocating joining a sports team or entering a marathon run just to build your network. What I am advising is that for people who already have these sporting or cultural skills, they can use these events not just for entertainment but also for getting to know more people.

The company's yearly barbecue or company picnic can be a similar opportunity to meet people from the wider organization that you would not normally have the opportunity to meet.

Internal training courses can also offer the opportunity to meet people from different parts of the organization. I personally benefited from weekly language lessons which enabled me to meet people whose working life couldn't have been further away from the department that I was working in. Learning a language together every week gave us a common interest other than work. As my career progressed and my role grew, I met these same people again but this time as work colleagues. Our existing friendships made it a lot easier to make the first professional contact and allowed us to work together with a good team spirit straight away. These people remained on good terms with me for many years to come.

During the length of people's careers, they are likely to change employers at some point. There may be many people that you have built good relationships with that leave the organization while you remain. When these people leave they are likely to share their personal email address with everyone they know or invite them to be friends on some form of social media. These connections can be very valuable and I would advise keeping their email addresses and remaining in touch. There are a number of reasons for doing this.

- You will need another job

- You may need a reference

- Sharing of professional information

If you need to leave your current organization then the people you know at other organizations can tell you what it is like to work for their employer, what roles are available there and they may even recommend you to their boss. Personal recommendations built trust and can "fast track" a candidate's entry into a new organization.

An ex-colleague of mine moved to a major competitor and some years later I applied to that competitor for a job. I didn't know that my friend and former colleague was working for the competitor. He was part of the senior management in the department that I applied to. He pulled out my CV from the huge number that had applied and personally recommended that they should hire me. As a result, I was one of the first to be interviewed, everyone that interviewed me knew that I had been recommended and they all trusted the manager that recommended me. They offered me the job.

Sometimes you need a referee for an application but you want to keep it secret from the people that you work with. If you remain in touch then this is a situation where you can ask an ex-colleague to be your referee. For example, this might be useful if you apply for a job outside your corporation and they want to check your references before you resign.

Another valuable use for good external contacts is when you need professional information from outside your organization. For instance, your employer may ask you to make a strategy recommendation. If you have only worked for this one employer and you don't have much knowledge of what other corporations are doing, then before making the recommendation you might have a private discussion with an ex-colleague to understand what their organization is doing. I am not suggesting that anyone shares company secrets. Merely that you contact the person you once worked with to get a wider view.

When to say "no" to extra work

Most managers have difficulty determining their staff's capacity for work. Most often, they will simply give you more work when you finish the work which you already have.

At times, when the pressure is on, then they will want the team to do more work. When this happens, the standard approach is for your manager to give you more work than usual on the expectation that you can stretch and find ways to get this work done. After all, everyone in the team is feeling the pressure and so they will want you to play your part. The team shares the load, everyone does more than usual, and the pressure reduces when the work gets done.

Be careful in this situation. Accepting more work and delivering good results is great, it will leave a lasting impression with your manager and with your team colleagues. Conversely, accepting more work during a period of work pressure and then not being able to deliver can be worse than having said no in the beginning. At least if you said no then your manager would have had the opportunity to consider who else could help. If it was important work, then your lack of delivery is likely to be remembered for a long time.

Therefore, it is important to know when to say "no", when to say "yes", and when to add risk reducing caveats. An example might be that you say "yes" on the understanding that in order to complete the extra work your colleague shows you how to do the task first.

Often the context is more complicated than the example given so far. For instance, you may have more than one person that gives you work to do. By stretching to deliver extra work for one person you might create conflict with the other person. In this situation it is important to explain your workload to your real manager (the one who conducts your appraisal and approves your compensation) and let him tell you if the work for the other people can go ahead or not.

If you feel confident that you can deliver, then a period of work pressure might also become an opportunity. Rather than waiting to be given more work you could volunteer to do a particular task that you wouldn't normally get to do and that could be beneficial to your career, perhaps a temporary increase in scope or responsibility

Can I be absent from work?

Your employer will have a policy that allows you to be absent from work that may include the following situations:

- Maternity
- Paternity
- Sickness
- Doctor's appointments
- Dentist appointments
- Holiday/vacation
- Bereavement

Your employer's company handbook or internal website will explain the policies around these different reasons for absence. What it will not explain is the social acceptance or the expectation of your colleagues towards whether these absences are taken or not.

When a woman is pregnant then she is likely to make full use of the maternity policy offered by her employer. There will still be some women who leave early and others who don't leave until the day they go into hospital, but this seems to be determined more by the risk to the baby and the mother's health than any social expectation. I have never heard of anyone being pressured to take less than the full maternity leave.

More and more corporations now also offer the fathers of newborn children a short period of absence. My personal experience is that fathers always take this benefit if it is offered, however, they will be influenced when they take it both by their family and by their current situation at work. For instance, I have known new fathers who were not in a position to stop what they were doing for 2 weeks and hence, instead, they took an absence of 2 days per week for a number of weeks to help their wife with the new baby.

Sickness is a much more complicated subject. There are typically two types of sickness benefits that are offered depending on the corporation. One type of policy offers a fixed number of days per year that can be used for sickness and when these days are used up then the employee must use their holiday/vacation days if they need to prolong their absence. The other type of policy is to offer an almost unlimited number of sick days with certain restrictions.

My experience is that corporations that offer a fixed number of sick days per year find that their employees make full use of all the days offered. That is to say that, the days are seen as a special type of emergency holiday by the employee that can be used for more than sickness. These days are always taken at short notice (as real sickness would be) and as a result, can be quite disruptive. I would also hazard a guess that employees with a fixed allocation of sick days end up taking more days off on average than those with unlimited sick days. The good news is that taking all the days within your sick day allocation is socially acceptable and I have not seen it being used as a yearly appraisal metric.

An unlimited sick day policy is quite different. The number of days may be theoretically unlimited but the controls around the use of these days are much tighter. For instance, within a certain number of days of absence, the employee must visit a doctor and get a medical certificate to prove that he is unable to attend work. Then if he is still absent after another few weeks then the employee will be invited to visit the company doctor who will decide, on behalf of the employer, whether this person is really fit for work or not.

It is certainly socially acceptable for people with unlimited sick days to have a few absences per year of a few days at a time or to have a full week's absence at some point. However, the total number of days taken is likely to be quite low on average unless the employee has a serious illness or attends hospital for a surgical procedure. Many people will be proud that they have not been absent due to sickness for a long period of time.

The bad news with the unlimited sick day policy is that the number of days taken each year is likely to have a role to play in your performance appraisal and in your compensation review. For example, if someone has had more than 2 weeks' absence due to sickness since their last appraisal then they are likely to have this point written in their new appraisal and they may need to explain the situation in their appraisal meeting. Also if the company offers performance-related bonuses then it is likely that the bonus will be reduced (prorated) by the number of days absent.

Of course, there will be times when you can't help yourself and you will need to take days off sick. The purpose of this section is simply to make you aware of the implications.

Keeping fit and healthy can reduce the number of sick days that you need to take. To help you with this, many corporates will offer access to a gym, or even yearly health checks. Find out which opportunities are available to you.

Holiday or vacation allowances can also be for fixed numbers of days per year or, in some cases, unlimited days. My experience is that unlimited vacation allowances are rarely indulged in fully by employees. These types of allowance are usually only offered when there is already a strong social pride in not taking much time off, as a result having unlimited holidays is purely theoretical because no-one gets to take long holidays in those corporates without damaging their career.

Be aware that in some corporates you need to accrue days before you can take them as a holiday. Therefore, when you start working for such a corporate you have zero days vacation in your holiday account. After 3 months you will accrue one-third of your annual holiday balance and so forth. As a result, if you are getting married in your first year of employment then your absence should be negotiated with them before your join.

What training is available to me?

A major corporation will have its own training department with its own catalog of available training. This may be part of the corporation itself or outsourced to a third party. It is likely to offer the following training.

- Business training
- Sales
- Public speaking
- Office tools
- Efficiency training
- Management
- Career appraisals
- Project management
- Languages
- Graduate training
- Fast track training
- Mandatory training

Business training will cover any training for the subject domain of the core business that the corporation is engaged in. There will be entry-level training that will be open to every employee and more advanced training that may only be accessible to people in revenue-generating roles.

Almost every corporation sells something to

external customers, whether that is services or products of some kind. Normally only the salespeople will be eligible to attend the corporation's sales training courses.

Public speaking courses can be wide and varied. Some will concentrate on how to make a presentation to a small audience and others may be more specialized such as how to speak to the external media. The entry-level courses will be available to everyone, and the more specialized courses will be restricted to people whose roles really require this training.

Training on office tools will be open to everyone. This includes training on spreadsheets, word processing, email tools, etc.

Efficiency training will be open to everyone and will include subjects such as time management, or managing meetings.

Management training is likely to be offered at many different levels. There could be a simple management course for new team leaders. Then there could be a multi-session course over a period of some months for more senior management. In addition, there could be a number of specialist management courses.

The HR department will probably run a course on how to prepare for and conduct career appraisals. In some organizations, this will be compulsory for anyone that has to conduct appraisals.

Project management courses are likely to be offered to anyone becoming a project manager or who has significant project management content within their role.

Some multinational corporations may offer foreign language lessons. Usually, the particular languages chosen are important to the corporate such as being the language used in their head office or in their major overseas subsidiaries.

Graduate training will be mandatory for all entrants on the graduate training program.

Eligible senior employees may be invited to join a specialist fast track training program that is designed to prepare people to become the high fliers of the organization.

In addition, there may be a number of mandatory training sessions that employees need to attend throughout the year so that the corporate can meet its regulatory goals. These could include anti-money laundering, anti-corruption, data privacy, and health and safety training courses.

You will have seen that some of these training courses are only open to people in certain roles, and other courses are open to anyone who wants to improve their skills. Within your first years in the organization, you may want to benefit from as many courses as possible to help you become better at your job and to ultimately make progress in your career. So one of the key questions is how much training are you allowed to have and how much training is socially acceptable within your team or department.

Your manager will hold a training budget. Before the last financial crisis, these training budgets were quite large and often they did not get completely spent from year to year. Since the financial crisis, many managers will have a much smaller training budget or even no budget at all. Despite this, there is still an employee expectation that they should receive training. For example, I can think of many people over the years who have told me that they expect to receive two training opportunities per year. I don't think I ever saw this written down anywhere but many people shared this same belief.

My advice is that the right training can be a good thing and can really help you to do your current job and to progress. I would propose that you get to understand the training policy of your employer and take a look at the courses on offer by the training department. Within your first few years at the corporation, if you know that your role makes you eligible for certain training courses then I suggest you apply for them directly or at least you discuss them with your manager and make him aware that you need them. These specialist courses are offered for a reason so don't leave it to chance that your manager makes the connection himself.

If you feel that they would benefit you, and you are not overbooked with specialty training courses, then I would suggest that you apply for some of the open-access courses too (e.g. public speaking or office tools). Your manager will have to approve all your training courses and he will certainly tell you if he thinks that you are asking for too much. Make it clear to your manager that by letting you attend these courses you will be more efficient afterward so the investment in time and money will be worth it.

Unfortunately, it is possible to fall into the trap of not attending any training courses for years on end. This can happen when you are very dedicated to your work, you know the area you are in has a high workload and perhaps your manager has made it clear that he wants the team in the office for as many hours as possible. You may get short term benefits from this approach, e.g. a good appraisal and performance bonus, but once it becomes normal then no-one will feel that you are making a sacrifice anymore and you will not be getting either the recognition or the training.

Knowing more about compensation

At some point, you are going to need to know what other people are being paid. Unfortunately, many corporations say that discussing your salary with other employees will lead to immediate termination of employment. This is difficult because if you don't know what your colleagues are being paid then how do you know if you are being paid fairly, and if you don't know what your manager is being paid then how do you know what you can aim for?

Some employees will discuss their compensation with work colleagues that they believe that they can trust. This might work for them, but they are taking the risk that the information is not the complete truth. A colleague may tell them a lower figure to avoid a complaint that could be traced back to them. Or a colleague may state a higher figure simply to create jealousy.

Alternatively, you could either ask a friendly

recruitment consultant or look for independent information on a website such as GlassDoor. The recruitment consultant will know very well the salaries for people he has placed but may not know the compensation for every role. GlassDoor is more independent, but it is worth testing some of their information for your organization before you fully believe it.

Regular reorganizations

Corporates, especially the well-known ones with lots of shareholders, don't tend to stand still for very long. You can expect that every five years there will be a major change.

- The trigger for a major change might be:
- Profits are down and cost-cutting is needed
- The corporate enters new business lines
- The corporate exits old business lines
- There is a change in top management
- Responding to reorganization elsewhere

In the reorganization, there will be winners and losers. Even when the reorganization is triggered by growth it is still possible that some people will lose their jobs or be forced to accept less attractive roles if they wish to stay. While at the same time, some people may gain more interesting roles or receive a promotion.

Unless the reorganization is dictated in detail from the top management then it is likely that working committees will be created to help design the new organization or to identify possible improvements. The people who are invited to participate in these committees will have to find the time in addition to their normal responsibilities (don't expect any help), but at the same time, they have the opportunity to build relationships with other departments and to learn in-depth how particular business lines work. Furthermore, only the best people are picked for these committees and therefore they will know that senior management is aware of them simply by virtue of being chosen.

If you are not chosen to be in one of the committees then the best you can do is to try to find out from your colleagues what is being discussed. Knowing the likely outcome of the reorganization may help you position yourself as an employee that absolutely must be in a key role within one of the new teams.

Surviving mergers and acquisitions

Corporations are likely to merge with other corporations or to be acquired by them seemingly without any warning. In practice, the top management will know full well if they are planning a merger and they will be having talks with the other corporation for months before they tell anyone in their own organization. I suspect they would also have some idea of being a potential acquisition target before it is discussed openly.

Mergers and acquisitions can be very stressful times for employees. In the beginning, very little information will be available and you won't know whether your job will be directly affected or not.

The first time a corporation that I was working for was involved in a merger, friends outside were telling me that I would learn more about what was going on from external news services than I would waiting for internal company announcements. I thought this was a joke until I realized that they were right. Reading the news to find out what is happening during a merger can be far more informative than waiting for your own company to make an internal announcement. My only thought as to why it appears this way is that the news services are prepared to publish rumors that they have gained from good sources, whereas your employer cannot risk telling you anything until it has been agreed to officially by all parties. This can cause quite a delay in communication.

There are several possible impacts on your role as the result of a merger or major acquisition. These could include.

- Redundancy
- Joining a larger team
- Changing roles
- Working in a smaller team
- No impact at all

In the extreme case, you may lose your job through redundancy after a merger or acquisition. If the new organization has publicly announced that it is going to reduce staff numbers as a cost-cutting measure then you know that redundancy for some people is going to happen. At this stage, I would advise trying to find out more about where the redundancies are likely to take place. For instance, this could happen in overlapping business areas or in areas where the new organization has no intention of continuing.

The merger or acquisition may increase the size of your department and you could find yourself working in a bigger team. This will create opportunities for some people to manage these larger teams but it could also mean that some managers get moved sideways if they don't get asked to run the new teams.

Long before there is any discussion about redundancies, you may be asked to join a new team with a new role. If you are being genuinely invited to do this based on merit then this could be a good move.

It is also possible that the department or team that you work in will be reduced in size and you could be offered a role in the reduced team. Again this will create opportunities for some people and sideways moves for others. For instance, in reducing the current team some people may be moved out and this could leave interesting roles open for existing team members to fill.

Not all managers are creative. Your new manager may have decided on your new role without thinking very hard about your skills or how the change will affect you. If you are unhappy then speak to your manager. Better still, research an alternative before speaking to your manager. Then he will see you helping him, by offering a solution, rather than simply complaining that you are not happy.

Revenue generating roles are less likely to be let go in a downturn. These are the roles that directly make money for the corporation (e.g. sales positions). The exception to this could be in a merger of equals when two competing businesses of similar size merge. The aim will be to reduce operating costs and, as a result, there will be less roles needed and even revenue generating roles are at risk.

As an example of what can happen when you ask, a friend of mine was working for a company in New York City when it was suddenly acquired by a competitor. His new manager proposed him a stable but uninteresting role. There were no other roles. Then, by speaking up my friend received a good severance package and was able to start a new career in Paris, France.

You could also find that there is no impact at all on your current role and responsibilities. This could well be the case if the business area you are in is seen as complementary to the other organization, in which case that department or team will continue as it is and could end up growing over time.

A colleague of mine was not comfortable with the uncertainty of the merger situation his employer had entered into. So he started actively looking for jobs with his employer's competitors. During one of his subsequent interviews, one of the interviewing managers shared some advice with him which is worth repeating here. He said that he had been through many mergers and found them less risky than changing employers. It takes years to build a good reputation and to be recognized, many people from the current employer will remain after the merger and you will still have that network. Moving to a new employer means starting all over again. My colleague took this advice and saw the merger through.

Imagine if you were one step ahead of the merger? This is possible if you join a merger task force. Senior managers will make the big decisions about company structure and headcount numbers post merger but they will leave the details of the team structures to the department heads and business line heads. These people are likely to invite existing employees to work in the merger task force to study the two organizations and make detailed proposals for department structures after the merger. You may be asked to join a task force or there may be opportunities to volunteer to join. Being invited to the task force is usually a good sign that your skills are recognized and that you will be retained.

Joining a merger task force is a lot of additional work, but you will have an enormous information advantage over your colleagues that would still be waiting to hear what will happen to them.

Raising concerns with your manager

There are many reasons why you might want to raise concerns with your manager, these include:

- You have issues with another team member

- You have issues with your manager

- You have issues with other teams

- Issues with your compensation

All of us will be in this situation from time to time. Therefore, the best way to approach it is to connect with your manager and build a relationship before you need his help. Then, when you ask for a meeting he will give you the time and when you start talking he knows that he can talk to you and he will listen. If the first real contact you have with your manager is when you raise an issue to him then you are already on the back-foot.

Even if you don't have an established connection, you could still consider asking your manager if he would like to join you for a coffee or to have lunch with you. That gives you the opportunity to build the very beginning of a relationship before launching into your issues. Then during the coffee or lunch start to open up about your issue. Also, this approach takes the edge of an issue by making it less formal so it would be suitable for discussing people or task issues but there are times when a more formal meeting would be better (e.g. you intend to resign).

When you do contact your manager with an issue then analyze the issue first. Certainly don't have this conversation when you are angry about what just happened and you simply want your manager to listen, he is not there for that.

Try to approach your manager with solutions not just issues. For example, we are having a problem with X and to solve this I suggest we do Y or Z for these reasons. In this manner you are making it much easier for him to make a decision (you have done the analysis) and he will remember that you are someone who comes with solutions not just issues.

This approach will work well in an open and productive work environment, if this is not the case or there are mitigating circumstances then consider a more formal approach, such as raising a grievance as explained in the next section.

Hard truth about raising grievances

If you have a problem with another member of your team who is at the same level as you, then if you can't resolve your differences the next course of action will be to escalate the issue to your manager. Or if you are having difficulties with your manager then your next step is to organize a specific one on one meeting with him.

By this stage you need to keep your own private written record of what takes place; include dates, times, key people and what was said. Print important emails for your records. If the subject was to blow-up and a third party comes to audit the situation then you need to show evidence of what has already taken place.

At this stage, the problem may be resolved quickly by talking to your manager. If not, and you feel that you can't put up with it any longer then you will need to escalate the problem still further and take it to your HR representative. Their first approach will be to attempt to resolve the problem informally between the HR representative and all the parties involved.

Maybe you feel that you are in a particularly bad situation and that there is no value in trying to resolve a problem informally then you can go straight to your HR representative and raise an official grievance. This will then be looked into by your HR representative. It will be recorded on your HR record that you raised this grievance and what the outcome of it was.

A grievance is not something to be entered into lightly. It is most often used by someone who feels that their issues are so great that they will not be able to continue working for that employer if their issues are not resolved. Only raise a grievance when you feel that raising a complaint to HR won't be enough. Frequently this path is taken when the employees' problem is with their line manager.

To understand how the grievance process is conducted we need to first look more deeply at the role of the Human Resource Department (HR). The HR team can be contacted for all manner of staff-related issues. Before approaching them with our issues we need to consider very carefully how they will react and whose side they will be on. Will they behave independently, will they defend the employee or will they take the company line?

There is an old saying amongst employees that the HR department's real purpose is to protect the company from its employees. This is seen by some people as being a negative statement about the HR department. Personally, I find it quite a practical way of looking at the situation and I will explain why.

Let us look at the alternatives first. Many people believe that HR is completely independent and fair. I am sure that many of them would like to be, but it is not going to be possible when their wages are paid by the company they work for not the employees. Furthermore, they need to have a close working relationship with the senior managers to whom they are assigned as their HR partners. They will not be rewarded for being altruistic. So there is little chance of them being truly independent.

However, imagine if a grievance was raised against the same manager that they need to have a close working relationship with. What if undeniable evidence arises during the grievance process that there is a real problem with the manager to whom the grievance was raised against and the matter could go to a court of law or an employment tribunal. In this case, there will be a point at which the HR team will have to stop supporting the manager in question. They would not stop supporting him because they are independent, we have already eliminated that option, but because their concern would then be how they could protect the employer from the rogue manager and how they could minimize the impact of the grievance that may now be upheld.

In conclusion, if you need a conflict resolved then you may need to raise it to your HR representative. This is a process. In the beginning, your grievance will be heard with an independent attitude, but as the grievance proceeds expect the HR team to side with your manager. Later on, if your grievance looks like it will be upheld then it will reach the point that the employer needs to be protected at the cost of the manager and the HR team may appear to be on your side again.

Whistle blowing

One other conflict resolution option is a whistle-blowing action. This cannot be used for performance-related issues or raising issues about your direct manager. It is used to inform on an action that took place that was not in the company's interest and from which the person raising the complaint needs to be protected. For example, if one employee sees another employee cheating a client then he could complain using the whistle-blowing process. If he was wrong and there was no harm done to the client then he would not be penalized for making the complaint because he would have been protected by the process.

The intention of the process is to allow employees to raise their concerns about situations that might otherwise hurt the corporation and to feel that they are free to speak with no repercussions.

How being mentored can help you

Many people benefit from having a mentor to help them with their career. Most CEOs and heads of business will have been mentored at some point in their career.

Typically a mentor is an independent person who is not part of your direct management line but is more experienced than you. The idea is that you can discuss what is happening in your career with this person and set goals for what you want to happen. The mentor can then help you evaluate whether you are going in the right direction to meet your goals and to help you come up with strategies to achieve it. You will be expected to do the work and the mentor is there to help you achieve it.

Some corporations have internal mentoring programs. Their HR departments may even match mentors to mentees. They are likely to target people who, with some assistance, could make it onto the management fast track.

If you think that this is something that you would benefit from but your corporation does not offer such a program then you could still look for someone internally who would help you on a voluntary basis or you could look for a mentor outside the organization. Some external mentors will expect to be paid and others will help you for nothing as they may have been helped in this way during their career.

Increasing your value to the organization

If you intend to have a long and prosperous career within your current organization then you need to look at the value you offer them today and what you could do to increase your value. Having a greater value compared to your peers should help you gain opportunities for career progression and at the very least should ensure you keep your job during times of hardship when other people are losing theirs.

These are some examples of things you could do to increase your value.

- International assignment
- Secondment to another department
- Business training
- Management training
- Become a mentor
- Learn a language
- Join an industry group

Having been on an international experience you

will be more valuable to the organization because you will know how the corporation operates in more than one place in the world. You will have also gained useful contacts in that area. A successful international assignment demonstrates to senior management that you are flexible and could be considered again for another assignment.

I can think of examples of many people who once they have started having international assignments they chose to continue to work overseas in different roles for the rest of their careers. I know of other examples where friends had a series of assignments overseas interspersed with periods back at headquarters in-between assignments.

A friend once explained to me that he worked for a Scandinavian multinational corporation. He had worked for them in one country but was not being offered the international roles that he wanted. He started to learn the language of the headquarters and soon after was offered a secondment to the headquarters. Once he had spent 3 years at the center of the corporation then he knew the key people and understood very well the culture and values of the corporation. Soon after he began to be offered the international roles that he sought.

A similar increase in value can be achieved by changing departments. Global corporations may operate in business line silos but they will also know the importance of having a few people who have worked in more than one area. Therefore if the opportunity arises, a person can add value by working in a different area for some time. This may be seen as a sideways move in the short term but in the long term, it could really help in obtaining a senior management position.

Knowing more about the company's core business will increase your value. I would recommend learning as much as possible from the people around you, from any internal clients you might have and from taking any business training courses that are offered. This is a necessity if you work in a revenue-generating role, but it is also of great value if you are in a support function. The key people in any support function should have a deep understanding of the real business of the corporation, not just expertise in their support area. When support functions are being offshored or outsourced, then having good business knowledge will be seen as a huge advantage. Remember that the knowledge of the business is one skill that external outsourced staff will not be able to offer.

Good managers are valued in any organization. If you have aspirations towards a management career path then take every opportunity to become a better manager. One way of doing this is to attend any management training courses that you are entitled to. Another approach would be to attend any management related talks that the company organizes. For instance, if you intended to be a project manager then listening to project managers from the construction industry who have managed huge building projects can be inspirational. Also, you could join an industry management body outside of work where like-minded people get together and share their experiences.

If there is an official internal mentoring program then you could volunteer to become a mentor. This would help you to meet people outside of your own immediate area. Also helping other people in this way is likely to help you to sharpen your own skills. Because it is the official internal mentor program then HR and senior management will know that you are helping other employees, so your effort would get recognition as well.

Global corporations, by definition, operate in many countries. Even if English is the common language of the corporation the local teams in each country will still speak their local language between themselves. Furthermore, if the headquarters of the global corporation is not in an English speaking country then the corporation will also have that language as a principal language. Learning this language can be the key to building relationships with people at the headquarters. It can also lead to a secondment to the headquarters which could be a good long term career move.

For a number of years in my career, I made a daily effort to learn the language of the headquarters. It enabled me to take roles at the headquarters where I managed teams who were not strong in English. As I progressed in both my career and my language skills, I was invited to meetings where no English was spoken and I ran steering committees without speaking English. Looking back on it, every member of the steering committee could speak English well and when I met with them one to one they often chose to speak English, but when they were all together in a room then they preferred to speak in their own language. I cannot say that I would have been barred from any of these roles if I could not speak their language, but I am sure that by speaking their language a level of confidence and trust was built which helped my career.

The downside of learning a language is that it takes a lot of energy and persistence over a period of many years. Therefore, you have to consider if this is a wise investment or whether you would be better spending time on more business training or more management training. The language itself may not be a transferable skill if you move to another corporation that does not use that language, however, learning a second language is also gaining the skills to learn further new languages. It is a personal choice.

It could also be of value if you joined an industry group. An ex-colleague of mine was an expert in a particular kind of banking communication technology. He volunteered to be the company's representative on the cross-industry committee to discuss the use and advancement of this technology. It was something he wanted to do and it added value to him and to the company.

Remember that ultimately everything is about sales. The corporation you work for needs to make sales to exist. Everyone in the organization should keep this in mind, it is not a subject just for sales-people. The most valuable things you can do will either protect the organization's sales (e.g. regulatory protection) or directly help the organization to get more customers, then sell more products and services.

Therefore, if faced with two options, always choose the one that is the most closely aligned with sales.

How office politics can affect you

Office politics is a power play where a group of people in the office use their position to gain some advantage which is often detrimental to the interests of the organization as a whole.

In any large group of people, some kind of politics is likely to take place. So office politics has its roots in normal human group behavior. How it differs in large corporates is that the potential rewards for a successful power play could be very attractive.

The desired outcome from office politics may include:

- Looking after their friends
- Currying favor with the department head
- Self-promotion
- Reinforcing team rivalry

In the simplest case, you may see office politics as no more than favoritism. Perhaps there is an industry event that everyone would like to go on. Then you find that the least deserving person has been invited but he regularly has coffee in a group with your manager's boss and so your manager chose him to please his boss. This is a minor case of office politics, it may affect the motivation of the team but no real harm is done.

Often office politics has the intention to obstruct rival teams. Imagine that two teams have different scope but they need to work together on some subjects in order to get their work done. When there is political rivalry, one team may avoid co-operating with the other team. This cooperation is likely to be based on goodwill and so they remove all goodwill. Typical situations include refusing to react to urgent requests and finding petty reasons to reject requests for cooperation. In public, they will, of course, claim to be cooperating and following the rules. Usually, this has no more value than to keep the rivalry going.

When office politics become toxic

When office politics are taken to excess then the workplace is often described as having become a toxic political environment.

The rewards sought by those engaging in toxic politics may include:

- Keeping their jobs
- Gaining end of year bonuses
- Removing other employees that could expose them
- Promoting people from their inner circle
- Influencing decisions

Those spending excessive amounts of time on office politics may well be failing in their real responsibilities of employment. They may have something to hide. They believe that by manipulating or threatening other employees, that they will not tell the whole truth to senior management and that will be enough to maintain the status quo. As a result, they will keep their jobs and influence. Instead, if the truth was to come out they may find themselves on a performance review or perhaps be sacked.

To achieve this manipulation they are likely to tell lies and create false rumors about the people that they want to manipulate. With their existing influence, they rely on being believed more than the person who is being manipulated.

In a similar way, the manager of a politically toxic team may make over-exaggerated claims about the team's performance that year believing that it will result in better compensation for him and his team. The problem with this is that corporates often have very interconnected teams and so by their claiming how well they have done it is likely to mean that another team must have done badly and risks receiving less compensation than they deserve.

This power play is also likely to rely on telling lies to senior management and having these lies believed. As this is aimed at discrediting a whole team then this is more audacious than discrediting one person and is likely to require a campaign over a period of months to tarnish the reputation of the other team.

A much easier manipulation for a manager who is engaged in toxic politics is to have one person removed that otherwise risks exposing him and his inner circle. At a junior level, they may simply find "dirt" on the individual that under normal circumstances would merit no more than a verbal warning, but in this case, they may instruct HR to put the person on performance review and then manage him out of the organization (quasi legally).

An alternative is to (incorrectly) grade someone very badly in an official career appraisal. After which the same performance review process can be followed. If the person targeted doesn't have a strong voice within the organization and doesn't have any influential friends then the power play will be quite easy for them to achieve.

If the toxic manager's team is larger than his own inner circle then he won't be able to resist "looking after" his inner circle to the detriment of other people within the team. He can promote anyone he wants within his team without any due process if he feels that it will benefit his cause. The people who are passed over for promotion within his wider team can only complain to HR, they are unlikely to have enough influence for it to be worth raising the issue outside the wider team and certainly not with the toxic manager. Unfortunately, if the toxic manager has a strong voice then HR will accept his opinion over the complaints of his wider team.

Another power play from the toxic manager could be to influence a major decision in order to gain some benefit for him and his inner circle. For example, a study may be conducted to choose between two external suppliers. The toxic manager and his inner circle may use their influence to ensure that their preferred supplier is chosen. They may then benefit by gaining some control over the supplier relationship or claiming credit for the deliveries of the external supplier. The supplier will not contradict them because they will have understood that they were only chosen due to the influence of the toxic manager.

The same toxic manager may choose to pay the staff that he favors more than his other staff. This typically means that he will skew the compensation review towards those in his inner circle or towards other people after which he will gain influence over them. This is not the behavior of a meritocracy. Up and coming stars that could challenge the toxic manager in the future may not be compensated fairly.

During an internal audit, someone within the organization is asked to review a particular area of activity within the company to grade the performance of the activity and to make recommendations. An audit of this kind is also open to office politics. Someone with influence can manipulate the people conducting the audit to determine the outcome. Possible motivations for manipulating the outcome of the audit include discrediting the people being audited or hiding evidence against their inner circle. Clearly, this manipulation of an audit wouldn't benefit the company in any way.

So how can you navigate your way through the pockets of toxic politics and get on with your own career? First of all, you need to be aware and notice when one of these situations is starting (see the checklist in the next section). Addressing it, later on will be more difficult (especially if your reputation has already been damaged). I would suggest keeping records of what is said that has the risk of turning toxic and collecting any evidence you can. Regarding your own performance, collect feedback from the people that you are delivering to. Also, this is where your own personal network will become invaluable, you may need people who can corroborate your version of events.

One other form of protection could be to communicate your own successes more often. It is difficult to attack someone's reputation if everyone knows that you are someone who delivers.

Escalating these toxic situations to HR is unlikely to benefit you. Those playing politics are usually clever enough to operate in the grey areas where there is no real truth, just one person's word against another. Remember that a toxic manager who is more senior than you is likely to have more influence over HR than you.

By now you may be thinking that if you ever find yourself in one of these situations then you would be better off joining them rather than trying to work around them. I would advise against it. To start with, it is likely to take years of complete subservience to be accepted into the inner circle of a group of people like this. Secondly, and more importantly, if you value openness, honesty, and meritocracy then you will find it hard to put aside your values to behave in the way that they would want. You could also console yourself with the question of how well these people would survive if they had to find a job outside in a new corporation where they would no longer have the protection of their toxic politics.

When you lose out due to office politics, then take the time to remind yourself how good you are. You may have been rejected for the promotion that you wanted, or you have had your work criticized, but if it is due to toxic office politics, then you will know that you only got caught in the crossfire. It is important to maintain your confidence and know that without politics, you would be dazzling management with your skills. It is just a temporary hiccup in your long career. Instead of dwelling on the unfairness, make plans for the future.

Toxic office politics checklist

If you have concerns that you are entering a toxic work environment then try the checklist below.

- Your manager has an inner circle that doesn't match team hierarchy.

- This inner circle meets regularly and for long periods.

- Your manager avoids committing to anything in writing.

- People outside the circle get poor appraisals.

- People outside the circle get passed over often.

- No cooperation with teams outside.

- Speaking alone with senior management is prohibited.

- Unexplained redundancies.

- Good performers on "last chance" improvement programs.

- High staff turnover outside the circle.
- No staff turnover within the circle.
- Speaking up is frowned upon.
- Important company information is not shared.
- Your manager isn't trusted by other teams.
- The company rule book doesn't seem to apply.
- Praise outside the circle is rare.
- Positive feedback from clients not shared.
- No opportunity to give feedback.
- Never invited to process review workshops.
- Manager is at war with other departments.
- No second chances outside the circle.
- Culture of fear.

You may have a toxicity problem in the workplace if a significant number of these tests are positive.

Crossing the Rubicon to management

Get recognized as a manager

If you have already taken the decision that you would prefer your career to go in the direction of managing, then to make that move you need to be recognized for your management skills before gaining your first opportunity to be a manager.

After you have declared your interest in management then senior management will be looking to see if you demonstrate the right skills for them to take the risk of giving you a management position. These skills would include:

- Amicable relationships with other employees
- Good communication skills
- Sharing your knowledge and helping other team members
- Supporting the management line (not being a rebel)
- Adding value to your current manager
- Being curious about the bigger picture
- Having confidence

However, observing any of these behaviors will work against you:

- Being late to work
- Being unnecessarily argumentative
- Gossiping
- Failure to do administrative tasks
- Sickness absence

Your first experience of management is likely to be within the scope of responsibility of your manager or his manager's scope. Remember that there is some truth that managers tend to promote people like themselves. This doesn't mean that you need to behave like a clone of your manager but you do at least need to have a good relationship and share some common ground.

Learn new skills

The value of good management is well understood, as a result, your employer is likely to offer many training opportunities for employees to eventually become managers (or to become better managers). Therefore you need to speak to your manager and apply for these training courses.

Similarly, you can ask other managers in the organization which internal training courses they recommend. Or even what books on management they recommend. Even though the training budget may be limited, books can be a good alternative.

There are also free and low cost training options that you can take up in your own time. For example, websites like Udemy offer a range of technical and management training courses with prices aimed at private individuals. Also, on YouTube you can find many excellent TED talks from industry experts on subjects such as management and innovation.

I remember that when I was at this stage in my career I was given the advice to silently watch my manager and consider what decisions I might make if I was in his shoes. When you know that your manager has a decision to make then do some research of your own and privately decide what you might decide to do before he announces his decision to the department. See if you reach the same decision, if not then consider why it was different. This is good preparation for thinking on your feet as a manager.

Managing within your sphere of knowledge

This is how most people get their first experience of management. You are already in the team and something happens that requires you to step up temporarily or permanently to run the team.

The last manager may have been promoted, suddenly taken sick or left the organization. Either way, that person's absence will create an opportunity for you to demonstrate your skills. If he was promoted, this could be the easiest situation because in that case the person is still around and may help you if need be.

Managing in a new area

When you manage people in a new area that you have never worked in before then that is when you truly cross the Rubicon.

Previously you might have become the manager of a team that you were once in, or became the manager of a very similar team. In such a situation you can use your in-depth knowledge to guide your management actions. You would already know the language, the business area, the tools involved and perhaps even the people themselves.

Then when you take over another team for the first time you have to rely on your management skills. There will be decisions to take very soon and you won't have time to learn everything in detail. Instead, you will have to work out very quickly who in the team can help you with what you don't know and start to build your plan. Often these opportunities only come up because something about the team needs to change, or they have a significant delivery to make and senior management didn't believe the last manager was capable of making the delivery. Rarely will you get the chance to take over a well-run team that just needs a new figurehead.

You are being tested. Prove yourself in this scenario and senior management will be left in no doubt that you are a manager and that they can give you other teams and services to manage.

Moving on

Always be prepared for change

You never know what is going to happen in the future. If your manager suddenly changes then it can make your days at work very different. It is a good idea to be prepared to make the most of the particular opportunities when they arise.

Remember that everyone is replaceable. You may think that because you are doing a good job, that you understand the business well, and that you know your way around the organization, that it will be difficult to replace you. Unfortunately, if senior management decides to downgrade your role and replace you with someone more junior for a lower cost or to eliminate your role (as part of a cost-cutting exercise) then they will. The time and productivity lost in someone replacing you will not stop anyone senior from sleeping at night.

If you have a personal plan with a personal set of goals and defined milestones then you can review every year whether you are getting there or not. If you aren't meeting your personal career goals then you need to think about what changes you could make in your career to correct this. I have met many people who have clear life goals and I was quite envious of the clarity they had of where they were going next.

Keep yourself up to date. This means both keeping your skills up to date, and keeping on top of what is happening in your industry. Think of this as an insurance policy. While everything is going well, you may be happy to keep your head down and deliver as much work as possible. If you take this approach, then when change comes, you will wish you may feel trapped, wishing you know more about what is happening in your industry and how the skills are changing. Instead, invest some time regularly in keeping yourself up to date, and then you will have confidence when facing change.

It is always a good idea to keep your CV up to date. You never know when you might need to look on the market for another role and when you do then you may have many more pressing things to do than updating the ten years missing from your CV.

Working at the same employer for years can reduce your ability to find roles and to succeed in job interviews. Recent practice makes a big difference. Many people find that when they start looking for a job after a long period that they don't quite make the grade for the first two interviews because their interview technique is not good enough. By taking more interviews they learn once again what needs to be done.

I remember a colleague who remained at the same organization for 10 years but he was always interviewing for other jobs. Because this person stayed for so long with the same employer I don't believe he was in a hurry to find another job. Instead, he enjoyed measuring his market worth and in every case, he must have been convinced all over again that he already had a good job. Someone like this will have kept their CV and their interview skills up to date and he would be fully prepared for the day that he needs to change corporations.

Part of being prepared can be to keep in contact with recruitment agents. You are likely to have met many recruitment agents either because they put you into the corporation that you are in now, or because they have tried to place you with other corporations since. Now as a mature hire your most likely route to moving corporations is with the help of one of these recruitment agents. They know which managers in which corporations are looking for staff. The best ones are also able to market you to their clients. For them to do this they need to know you.

The question then is whether you need to keep in contact with recruitment agents, even when you are not looking for a role, so that they know about you and can market you better. To answer that we have to also look at whether the recruitment agent will want to keep in touch with you.

A recruitment consultant will genuinely want to keep in touch, not so that he can market you but because he will want information from you and for you to appoint them to recruit staff for you. Your corporation may not have this recruitment consultant on its preferred supplier list and therefore you may not be able to use them to recruit for you. In which case the only currency you have to offer is information. So if you keep in regular contact with recruitment agents then expect them to regularly pump you for information on who you might know that would meet their current candidate searches. You will have to decide if this is the price worth paying.

Reasons for leaving

It is unlikely that you will work for one employer for the whole of your career. Here a list of possible reasons why you might leave.

- A better opportunity
- Retirement
- Redundancy
- Ill-health
- Getting fired

The most common reason to leave a corporation is to take up a better opportunity elsewhere. It will be you alone that decides what "better" means in this case. It could include finding a role with higher compensation, a major promotion, moving to a better activity area, moving countries or getting away from something that you don't like in the current organization. Leaving in this way requires you to resign from your current employment contract.

After resigning, you would need to continue to work during your notice period as defined in the employment contract and then you would be free to leave. Alternatively, in some customer-sensitive roles, an employee may be asked to leave the office immediately after their resignation has been accepted. They would still have to wait for their notice period to end before starting work for their new employer but they would have to spend their notice period at home. This is typically referred to as "garden leave".

If you have reached the company retirement date then you are likely to leave for retirement and start drawing your pension. In some countries, you are allowed to work past the official retirement date, although not all companies will support this. In most cases, the employment contract would automatically terminate on the date of retirement unless a contract waiver was signed to prolong the contract past the retirement date.

Another common reason for departure is redundancy. This is where the corporation decides that it no longer has a role for you and as a result, it terminates your contract of employment by reason of redundancy. In this instance, the corporation is likely to pay compensation to the employee that at least matches the legal minimum defined within the country where they are working.

If someone suffers from ill-health, and there is no sign of this improving, then that could also lead to them leaving the corporation. Before this happens they may officially be on long term sick leave where they remain legally an employee of the corporation. If the situation is not going to improve then rather than remaining on long term sick leave forever they may reach a mutual agreement with the corporation that they should leave. Legally, people do not terminate employment contracts for reasons of ill-health. Therefore the legal reason for departure will be resignation or redundancy depending on the situation.

If an employee has behaved badly then his contract could be terminated for reasons of gross misconduct. This could include breaking company rules, failure to follow strict compliance rules, breaking market regulatory rules or becoming convicted of criminal activity. The termination of the contract would be immediate with no notice period or compensation of any kind. This is not very common. I can only think of a very small number of people that I know have been fired during my career.

What is a better opportunity?

How do you know for sure that a role in another organization will necessarily be better? Remember the saying that the grass is always greener on the other side, there is a risk of being flattered by the opportunity. You should research the opportunity and look for suitable evidence to support your decision.

If your only reason for moving is compensation, then don't just look at the short term gain you will achieve by moving but instead look at the longer-term compensation opportunities. For instance, if you are going to receive a 5% increase in total compensation by leaving then think about whether if you stayed would have got that 5% increase in the next compensation review anyway. If you have evidence that the company you want to join consistently pays higher compensation as seniority increases compared to your current employer then you may be making a good long term move.

Remember also that people tend to inflate their own personal compensation in conversation. So when your friends tell you that they are all earning significantly more than you then keep your jealousy in check until you can verify their figures.

Casual verification can be achieved by finding other people you know in your network who have worked for that corporation or still do work for that corporation. Of course, the real verification will come when you are offered a job by that corporation but that could take some considerable time which will have been a waste if you attended interviews on a false understanding of their compensation amounts.

Earlier in the book, we also mentioned finding out salary information from recruitment consultants or through websites such as GlassDoor.

Much of the advice given at the start of this book on selecting an employer and finding a job for the first time should be revisited at this point to make sure that the move you are thinking about still makes good sense. The difference being that now you have started work you will have a much better understanding of what matters to you than you did before. For instance, it is easy to think that we can work 24 hours per day in our first job, but when you work 18 hours per day for months on end then you might have a different idea of how many hours you want to work at any future position.

For those in a management position looking to get ahead, a stepping stone to a much better opportunity could be to enroll on a full time MBA course. Once you have had at least one serious experience of being a manager then you will have the background necessary to get the most out of an MBA from a practitioners point of view.

How to survive the redundancy process

Redundancy can happen to anyone who is employed and it can happen at any time. Often when it happens it comes as a shock and the period immediately following redundancy can be very stressful. All corporations are different and different countries have different employment laws. However, it may reduce the stress of the situation to know how redundancy works so here follows an explanation of the sort of process that a redundancy is likely to follow.

The first you will know of the redundancy is when you are called to a meeting by your HR representative and you notice that your manager is also present. Between the two of them, they will read from a pre-prepared script announcing that your job is at risk and that you have now entered a period of consultancy with the corporation. At the end of the period of consultancy if you haven't been accepted for another role within the organization then your contract will be terminated. This first meeting will be very short and very official. Don't expect any long explanations at this stage. Often the consultation period is one month.

Depending on the corporation, you may be offered the opportunity to go home for the rest of the day to take in what has happened and to think about what your next move will be; if this isn't offered then you could ask for it. Before you leave the meeting you are likely to be informed as to whether you are expected to attend the office during your redundancy consultation process or whether you can stay at home. Attending the office means to continue to do your day job, this may give you the opportunity to network with people and to find another role but it also means that you will be very busy. If you have the chance to stay at home then it is unlikely to mean that you can't come into the office, instead, you can probably come and go as you wish which will give you the most freedom to network internally and externally. You need to be clear on this point before leaving the meeting.

Following the first meeting, you will be issued with a letter that will again inform you of the risk of redundancy and stating that a period of consultancy has started. The letter is likely to contain exactly what was said during the meeting with HR but it is likely that you will notice a lot more detail in the letter as there would have been a lot to take in during the meeting itself.

You will then be invited to the first of many HR follow up meetings with your HR representative. The purpose of these meetings is to ensure that the corporation can say that it has made all reasonable efforts to find you another role. It is up to you to use these meetings to help you get another role. If you don't make much of an effort then the HR representative will not push you into another role. On the other hand, if you ask the HR representative to make introductions for you or ask certain managers about vacancies then they will happily do that for you because to not do so would imply that they had not taken reasonable effort to find you another role.

On a weekly basis, you are likely to receive a list of all the job roles the corporation has open in your city of employment. If you are interested in opportunities in other cities or overseas roles then ask for these lists too. Although, remember that any overseas roles will be on local contracts with no expatriate assistance.

You can apply for these roles yourself or you can ask your HR partner to help. The advantage of involving the HR partner is that they may have the power to influence the selection of candidates. Sometimes senior management set targets that could lead to your HR person pushing your application to the top of the pile, it does happen.

If you find another role internally and you accept the role, then your redundancy consultation period will immediately come to an end and you will remain fully employed. There is a possibility that your compensation will be reviewed (up or down) for the new role, other than that everything will stay the same.

Alternatively, if you don't find another role within the consultation period then your HR representative will inform you that you are now redundant. Within 2 or 3 days your employment contract will then be terminated and any redundancy compensation will be paid to you. During those 2 or 3 days, you will have the opportunity to clear your desk if you have not already done so. Remember that on the day that the contract is terminated then any benefits you receive (e.g. health insurance) will also be canceled.

Following the termination of your employment contract, you will be immediately free to join another employer without serving any notice period.

Losing your job in this way has a different effect on different people. For some people, their personal identity is so linked with their job that they feel redundancy is a loss similar to the death of a friend and as a result may grieve this loss for some period of time. Other people may see it as an opportunity to start a new challenge elsewhere.

Conclusion

This book has covered major topics to get the most out of your current corporation and different ways to plan for your departure at the end.

We spend such a large portion of our waking hours at work that it is worth making your career what you want it to be. Your job should make you happy, leaving you satisfied and fulfilled. A successful career is rarely about just power and money.

I sincerely hope that this book helps you with your career and I wish you all the best for the future.

Clive Verrall

About the Author

Clive Verrall has had a career spanning more than 30 years. During this time he worked in the financial industry for more than 20 years, much of it for a global banking group with more than 200,000 people.

He has lived and worked in 4 countries and traveled for business to more than 20 countries. During his career, he has risen from graduate entrant to Chief Operating Officer and every role in between.

At the time of writing, Clive Verrall lives in Asia working on startups that he has invested in and writing books.

When it comes to writing, Clive Verrall specializes in non-fiction, writing about his experiences and those of the people that he has met.

The author can be contacted from his website: (https://cliveverrall.com/contact)

Find out more about the author and his current book projects at (https://cliveverrall.com/books)

Other books by this author

1: *What you need to know before joining a big corporate*

This book is for people with ambition that want to join a big corporate and to make it their career.

Working for a corporation can be very rewarding financially and professionally. You could find yourself working with very bright people from all over the world and gaining experiences that change your perspective on life. Big corporates continue to offer permanent contracts, training, overseas experience and the opportunity to increase your starting compensation 10 times.

Any previous employment is unlikely to have prepared you to work at a big corporate. A multinational corporate may have more than 200,000 employees globally, with offices in every major city across the world. Its corporate culture is a closed environment with a structure and rules that are not known outside.

There will be a lot to learn to navigate the organization while at the same time meeting your daily responsibilities. Like you, everyone who joins a major corporation wants to succeed. The rewards are high and so is the competition. The corporations themselves won't teach you how to succeed and therefore the difference between a successful career and a frustrating early departure will depend on how well you can find out this information for yourself. This book will help you.

2: *Essential introduction to Investment Banking Information Technology*

What do you need to know to become successful in investment banking IT? How does investment banking IT work, what are the essential concepts and the critical IT systems? This book is aimed at anyone in IT who wants to increase their understanding of the rewarding world of investment banking IT. It will be of benefit both to people who know very little about investment banking and want a complete introduction to gain entry and it will also be useful to those who already have experience and want to get a robust understanding of the subject to accelerate their career.

Investment banking is a complicated collection of subjects. It is no surprise that the IT systems built for investment banking can also be complicated and are often implemented only by people who have an in-depth understanding of a particular niche of the investment banking business for which the system is needed. This in-depth knowledge takes years to accumulate and as a result, IT staff with that knowledge are hard to find and are well paid. This makes it difficult for newcomers to break into this large and still growing IT area or even to switch domains within a bank once they have already started. In this book, I will share my experiences gained over more than 20 years to fast track the reader's career.

Throughout the book, investment banking activities are explained in the context of what their demands on the IT department are. For each activity area this includes looking at system diversity, IT team sizes, IT process maturity, technologies used, key IT roles and whether advanced mathematical skills are needed.

3: *Achieve Personal Success in Enterprise IT Offshoring, Outsourcing and Captive Centre Management*

You may be involved in offshoring today, your employer may have told you it is planning to offshore or you may have been asked to evaluate a company's strategy which includes offshoring. You may have heard that offshoring saved one organization millions of dollars but simultaneously another organization is mysteriously reducing its outsourcing. But what does it mean and are these subjects comparable?

Offshoring is a huge subject. It has its unique vocabulary and its own set of specific skills that are not part of the mainstream. It has its own models and life cycles. It is a product of the "flat world" and the interconnected global economy that we now live in. If you want to understand the practicalities of this subject to ensure your personal success in offshoring, outsourcing, building an offshore center, or in setting IT strategy or you are just curious about lifting the lid on this vast subject then this book will help you.

The book focuses on the offshoring of IT activities from corporate IT departments to their offshore facilities or an outsourcing vendor. It will also give examples of how this extends to cover non-IT Business Process Offshoring activities. This book includes advice and lessons learned from real offshoring experiences. This is not a book about statistical trends in offshoring or untested management theory.

4: *Raising your internet business: How to deliver successful web projects for your small business*

Do you want your business to be among many businesses that thrive and expand due to their successful online business models? Many of these businesses derive the majority of their revenues from internet customers whom the businesses will never meet, or from customers who find the businesses online and then visit the businesses' physical premises.

How do these businesses attract these customers? These opportunities are only possible if your business has an online presence. How do I put my business online? What services should I offer? How will I accomplish all of this on a small business budget? You may have a vision of the website you would like to have, but as a small business owner, you probably won't have an IT department to which you can delegate this project responsibility. You can hire experts to help you, but you won't know how to supervise them unless you first gain an understanding of the key subjects involved. How can you negotiate a good deal unless you already know the advantages and pitfalls of putting your business online?

As a web professional, I have regularly been asked these questions by my myriad clients. Usually, I only have time to give clients a quick answer, and not enough time to explain everything I'd like. This book contains the more comprehensive answers that I would like to have told my clients, and from which any small business reader can now benefit.

Put all these explanations together, and this book

gives you the essential information you need to get your business online.

Visit (https://cliveverrall.com/books/) to find out more.